John Corbett

Codd's
CONCORDANCE

The A-Z of one farmer's philosophy

John Codd
Illustrations by Jean Thomas

Conna Publications

Published in 2009 by Conna Publications
Haverfordwest, Pembrokeshire SA62 6HF

ISBN 978 0 9563839 0 7
A CIP record for this title is available from the British Library.

Printed and bound in Wales at
Gomer Press, Llandysul, Ceredigion.

For Rhiannon and Jennie

Dedicated to the memory of
Sandy Mowers

whose wisdom and guidance has
inspired my philosophy

Foreword

The Oxford Dictionary definition of 'character' reveals the word's many variants. Applied to us as human beings, our individual idiosyncrasy, mental or moral nature, strength, backbone, reputation and qualities or testimonial status are all included. More specifically, it can be taken to refer to a well-known or even an eccentric person.

The word is multifaceted. So too are those people we know within our communities simply as 'characters'. John Codd is undeniably a member of that select band and almost invariably referred to as such at the very mention of his name. He displays many of those facets and, in this little book, brings together a collection of musings and thoughts that are the living embodiment of this.

They are the product of an agile and perennially active mind whirring away in the close company of his cows in past years, whilst working the land or else merging into the countryside with a gun on his arm and a dog at his side. As his closest neighbour and one of his legion of friends, I know that they have all been explored and shared with many of us sitting alongside the range at the Gwachal, embellishing his customary hospitality.

This little book is an opportunity for everyone to share in these original thoughts, to be provoked by them, perhaps to see a different slant on things that are otherwise unexceptional, being free to adopt or contradict them. Most of all, it is something to pick up and enjoy.

Terence John
September 2009

Acknowledgments

I wish to thank my family, friends and the people I have met on the road in life who have all had an input into my philosophy, both 'good' and 'bad'! Without their input there would be nothing I could offer you. Please feel free to take as much or little as you wish.

Codd's

$\mathcal{A}$ = Always

Always enjoy the wet days.
There will be plenty of
dry ones after
you are long dead and gone.

$\mathcal{B}$ = Be sure

Be sure to remember where you
are before you start anything in
this life otherwise you will spend
your time going round in circles.
You can only go south if you
know which way north is.

C = Count

Count your blessings they say.
I do. I also count my losses
and my misfortunes.
I count the good and the
great in this world.
I also count the pain and the
injustices in this world.
I accept it all. I will live my life
accepting all that it has to offer
and will make the best of it
and will be prepared to be judged at
the end of life by the
sum total of my life.

D = Deny

Deny yourself and you
are only fooling yourself.
Life is too short.
I do not think you
get a second chance.
If you miss a chance it will never
present itself again.
One day more is one day less.
Make the most of
what life has to offer.
Take each and every day
and be thankful for
all it has to offer.

E = Embrace

Embrace today,
you can relive yesterday but
you can never recapture it.
Remember and live on.
Or should it be live on
and remember?

Codd's

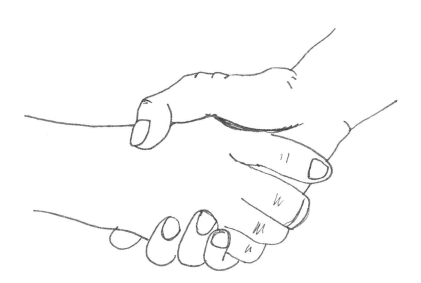

F = Friendship

Friendship should never
be given lightly.
Never offer anything which
you cannot fulfil.
Circumstances change and your
ability to fulfil your obligations alters.
Do not forsake your friends.
You never know when your needs
will be greater than theirs.

G = God

God gave you two ears
and one tongue.
Therefore listen twice as much
as you talk.
I guarantee you will be a wiser
person if you do and when you
do talk people will be more
prepared to listen to you.

My father's advice to me.

H = Helping

Helping those worse off than yourself is a very noble deed although it might not appear to be the most profitable.

But remember your rewards in this life are not always obvious.

I = Invite

Invite your enemy to dinner.
You never know when
you may have to eat at his table.

J = Judge

Judge others with the same
intensity and standard
with which you yourself are
prepared to be judged.

K = Kind

Kind words take the same thought and effort to utter as harsh and cruel ones but they often appear harder to say.

L = Life

Life is like a train journey.
The distance travelled is immaterial.
What counts is the quality of the
scenery you pass on the way.
Too many people live their life
like riding in a train carriage going
through a tunnel never aware of the
outside world and all it has to offer.

M = Make

Make your own destiny in this world.
You are not always responsible
for the situation you find yourself in
but you have the power to
influence the outcome of every
scenario if you believe in it enough.

$\mathcal{N}$ = Never

Never regret your mistakes,
for they are part of life which made
you what you are today.
The only mistake anyone made
was the one they did not learn from.

Codd's

O = Only

Only ever look down on those people who look down on you. Remind them and yourself we are all equal in the grand scheme of things.

ℙ = People

People say the grass is always
greener on the other side but they
never ask, was there any grass
left in the first field?
The circumstance of life is not
always as obvious
as it may first seem.
Was greed or starvation
the motivation?

Q = Question

Question your own
beliefs and ideas,
with the same thoroughness
that you question
those you disagree with.

Codd's

R = Rain

The rain on your back
is always preferable
to the sunshine
on your grave.

Codd's

S = Show

Show respect for those
who respect you,
for it is they that
deserve it the most.

Codd's

T = Take

Take the time to study and understand the things you do not like or understand.
You will be surprised at the answers you will gain. And be prepared to change your own views.

U = Understand

Understand your weaknesses.
It will help you build on your strengths but, remember, that which you consider a weakness those around you may well consider to be your strength.

V = Value

Value is always proportional
to the volume and quantity of the
substance in question and the area
in which it is measured.

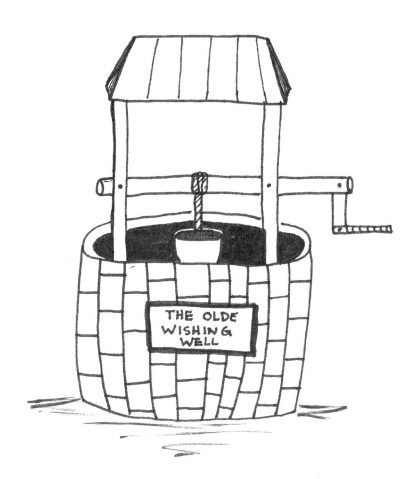

THE OLDE
WISHING
WELL

W = Wish

Wish only for the things in
this life that there is a possibility
of achieving.
Wishing for the impossible
will lead to despair and frustation
which can only achieve
disillusionment with your life.

Codd's

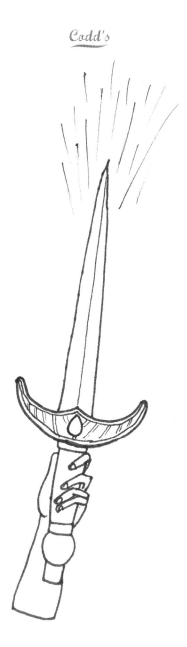

X = Xiphoid

Xiphoid defines resembling a sword.
A sword has uses both
symbolically and literally.
It can represent power, justice,
aggression, defensiveness, or pure
practical use such as
cutting one's bread.
Therefore, always look at every
interpretation of a situation or word.
Do not reach a conclusion from the
first thing you see, read or hear.
Try to gain all the facts before you
react or voice an opinion.

Codd's

$\mathcal{Y}$ = Yours

Your financial and material gains in this world will allow you to take out of this life the same amount you came into it with. Nothing.

Z = Zebra

A zebra born without stripes
would be called a horse.
It is only the circumstance of birth
which gives one
advantage over another.
Do not feel superior to someone
born less fortunate than yourself.
They could have been you,
and you they.

Codd's

CONCORDANCE

Codd's